No Names Have Been Changed

ALSO BY SIRIOL TROUP

Drowning up the Blue End
Beneath the Rime

Siriol Troup

No Names
Have Been
Changed

Shearsman Books

First published in the United Kingdom in 2017 by
Shearsman Books
50 Westons Hill Drive
Emersons Green
BRISTOL
BS16 7DF

Shearsman Books Ltd Registered Office
30–31 St. James Place, Mangotsfield, Bristol BS16 9JB
(this address not for correspondence)

www.shearsman.com

ISBN 978-1-84861-544-1

ACKNOWLEDGEMENTS
Thanks are due to the editors of the following publications where
many of the poems, or versions of them, first appeared:
*Horizon Review, Magma, Modern Poetry in Translation, Mslexia,
New Welsh Review, PN Review, Poetry London, Poetry Review,
Poetry Wales, The North, The Warwick Review.*

My thanks also to Anne Berkeley, Claire Crowther,
Lorraine Mariner, Sue Rose and Tamar Yoseloff
for their invaluable advice and friendship.

Contents

for Edward

Looking for Bitterns

If I could start from scratch
it would be here on this winter marsh,
grey wind shucking the lichen
from blackthorn and elder, everything
hunkered down, kipper-brown and husky,
reeds standing their ground,
liverworts ironed onto the shingle.

It's the same in the hides: dogged
lines of bobble-hats and scopes,
a fixity of purpose that goes beyond
requirements. A bittern flew in earlier,
neck tucked back, legs trailing like ferns.
Now it teases through the veils of sedge
existing because they believe in it –
the foghorn boom, the khaki camouflage.
They'll wait for dusk to fall,
the water's feathers to smooth.
This is how it begins.

We heard the ravens shriek at dawn

Once upon a time
huge forests grew along our coasts:
thick stands of larch and ash,
flickers of mossy shade,
logs, kindling, circular saws,
somewhere or other
a body for dissection.

We followed the trails, silent, on edge.
We weren't alone –
you with your gun cocked,
an expression of pure Romanticism.

The forests rose behind.
Streams roared down the slopes.
Trees and fruit had come to an arrangement.
Ravens perched on the spikes,
ponderous, glossy, short of breath,
shimmering, glittering plumes.
Foxes, martens, adders, nuthatches, stags…
What gender were the pines?

Oh, my craving for bilberries –
light dwindling to a thread,
leaves in colours spun from green air.
Then summer passed, and autumn too.

Was it so hard for us to show our feelings?
How long were the shadows we had to leap?

Via Flaminia

Lightning flickers on the hills, wasps
crater the plums. Madness to leave
the superstrada striking through the cliffs
and take this cranky Roman pass
cut deep in the gorge – the little forum
where we find ourselves ducking
the sun's aim, strung along sheer rock
by engineers of hope while time traps
Vespas and Vespasian in its flow.

Beyond the river's chloroform bend
the land smells of polecats,
woolly oaks, yellow-bellied toads.
Shivered with spray, the future roars.

Dover to Margate

Thick fog fallout, a tumble
of badger guts frosted on the kerb.
One black shoe in the fast lane,
cars ahead reduced to two red eyes.
Shops barred, tills mute, salt-stores plundered.
Arrows on the pavement THIS WAY FOR CREDIT.
New Meridian villages without a soul,
fields of heartbroken cauliflowers.
A battery of laid-up ships marking the face-off
between sea and sky.
                        Are these the dangers
warned of on the signs,
chilling enough to make us turn
into the spit of the wind, the wind lifting
kite and gull over white cliffs and crazy-golf
towards a dreamland rising past the next
lifebelt, the next lighthouse, the next
headland, the next wave, the next
godforsaken bay?

New Iceland

Gimli, Lake Winnipeg

The town is winter-struck:
propellers jammed, fishing-boats on blocks,
lake a frozen abstract –
white blue grey blue white,
coastguard-cutter bobbing, bobbing
like an ice-hut over ink.
Blood warms itself on cloudberry pancakes
and the murals on the harbour wall.

In the Heritage Centre, crops fail
and fathers drown.
Dying children can't be saved by knitting
or a reading from the sagas.
Mothers write psalms in the snow
and watch their lives skate by on runners.

No one remembers the long nights
when wind riled the turf,
the smell of whale oil and wool,
the old life thrashing in nets
while the ones who cut loose
believed they were rowing to heaven.

Homemaking in the West Reserve

In heaven, where the body is raised
to infinite airiness, they have no need for beds.
Here, in a place of honour in the living-room
the *heaven-bed* with its panelled sides,
flamboyant scalloping and well-turned pediments
is stacked to the ceiling with blankets
like a test for the real princess.
The higher the pile, the better the prospects,
the thicker the covers, the warmer the welcome,
the snugger the guests, the higher the life ...
and so on and so forth, through twenty
counterpanes and quilts. Is is all about status,
this display-case for towering domestic skills?
Hard to tell when the layers are held down
by a handmade veil and the look of a bride
cautioned since adolescence
that pride cometh before a fall.

Yellow Rain

for Paul Bergman

Today I found drops of cream on the garden table
as if the world were upside-down and clouds were cows.
Close up the rain was full of sand, a desert
whirled aloft by ghibli winds and set down
here among the lilacs and tulips.

Later your sweetgrass verses dropped out of the blue
bringing home my daughter pouring milk in her tea
in the town where your forefathers planted their fields.
Yellow dust swirls through the corn.
She sips and smiles, she smiles and sips.

Raspberries at Dusk

Night draws down, draws
no distinction between shapes and gaps,
smoothing the landscape into sombre parataxis.
Stone cat vanishes through metal
grass, pond-eye seals its lid.
Field respects a new democracy:
shrubs are figures, figures
fences, fences trees,
trees abstractions of themselves.
Fingers find the gate's latched
breath, its sullen rust, the easy berries
dropping with little sighs
like sins relieved. We are all the same
in the dark. The light discovers
mildew, fruit-worms, stains on every hand.

Stealing Daffodils

They were standing there asking for it,
heads like sounding brass,
stems as fat as charity,
great clumps of them close to the fence,
big mouths crammed with fresh air
from the better end of town.

On a cold Sunday in Lent
they were the devil's flowers
flashing between the gaps,
solid, buttery, wanton as plastic.

Remember the shock of that first snap,
the drool of spit on your hand.
How, out of the ground
they seemed too rain-blown
for even the cheapest bouquet.
How they came so easily
it never felt wrong.

Virgin for short but not for long

Where would it all end – dead cows,
riots, flames dropping out of the sky?

We spent a lifetime in the basement
while our parents raged.
We stole their filter-tips, got drunk on Advocaat,
threw up in curious yellow on cream suede.

Virginia met a rock-star living in a squat.
She left me tarot cards, her incense-burner
and *The Joy of Sex*.
I wore her Afghan coat and see-through tops.

I counted days, then months. The lies I told.
The dog, run over by a lorry, wagged
his broken tail, sprayed blood on every wall,
messed up the whiter shades of pale.

My father plans to meet me on the other side

He's been meeting me for years:
stations, airports, docks,
Kuwait, Berlin, Benghazi, a field once
near Maastricht, full of startled cows.

His shadow through glass.
His smile opening doors and duty-free.
His half-salute –
four fingers and a stump of thumb.

And time cracking the tarmac
like phantoms or harriers.

His faith is everlasting:
Queen and Regiment, the BBC,
the healing powers of cabbage-water,
David Niven's heaven.

I know the form:
he'll pace the halls and check
the empty gates, holding his breath,
tapping his walnut stick,

praying I'll change the ending
where he waits and waits.

Discipline

I dreaded the shadowy path,
the cypresses from *Island of the Dead*,
the musty biscuits on a Meissen plate.

Halfway through term Frau Stiel suggested
Middle High German might be beyond me
but we agreed to soldier on.

Meticulous, dogged, monotonously instructive
she gave herself to ground-breaking,
vowel-shaking upheavals:

the first and second consonantal shifts,
a-mutation, u-mutation, isoglosses trenching
High from Low and North from South,

Gutenberg, Luther and Grimm,
battles between the scripts, the semantic shudders
of Nazi ideology, alphabets unravelling.

None of which prepared her for the day
her daughter stabbed a shop-assistant in the heart,
a pin-prick in the slow evolution of Germanistics

but shock enough for fricatives to quake.
Police at the door, lives slamming shut.
No more biscuits, no more pretty plates.

Hitler on Heligoland

23rd August, 1938

How many of the island's fishermen
watching him beach at the edge of their rock,
a flap of arms, brass glinting like scales,
remembered nets hurled back
when haddock or whiting parted to reveal
a creature from the ocean's darkest zone,
brownish-black, ugly as sin, though smaller
than its names and reputation might suggest:
fangtooth, triple-wart sea-devil, loose-jawed
dragon-fish, vampire squid from hell.

Extremities

It started as a bruise, a run-in between foot
and door, a black spot on her big toe that bloomed
into a scaly growth the doctor said
would take a year to cure.

Now it's cutting its teeth on the pearl of the nail,
a Rorschach blot that throws up
peglegs and crutches, tomorrow polished off
by the imagination's barracudas.

Border Dogs

Freedom in no man's land
was a hundred metre flexi-leash that ran
on trolley-lines between the trip-wires
and the beds of nails: technology matured
to perfection – no built-up slack, but room
to roam. We learned to keep the rules.
No pissing in the fields of fire, no fouling
of the death strip or the Stalin lawn.

Exercise never felt less of a strain.
We leapt at whispers, sniffed out pointless
acts of courage. Meals were thrown in,
choc-drops for injuries or amputations,
shadow-play to keep us on our toes –
puppets dangling on the white wall
tangled in their strings, exits
and entrances that left us gasping.

When watchtowers went blind and lights
stopped searching, we sat on our tails
while colour poured across the ramparts.
Who would cut us loose?
We shut our eyes and raced to the end
of the track, counting on cold-war
practicalities: sudden pull-back
and a quick release.

Emancipation

YIELD it said in six-foot letters on the runway.
I crossed the paranoia boxes, surrendered
iris-patterns at the gate.
A denim sky hinted at the conquest of infinity.

I entered the free world through a tunnel of eyes,
arms up, nothing in my pocket
but a white tissue
my ghost flagged up to cosmic radiation.

Provocateur

As I cross the bridge
a young man clings to the railings
muttering *Kleist* or is it *Christ*?

In Committee Room 15
Britannia flashes dread-and-envy hair
and late-Diana eyes
as she forks through the mess
dropped by civil servants.

I keep my head down,
bury my thoughts in the files,
play dead while she tortures
the pedants. Here's *my* manifesto:
axe-heads and woad, hand
to hand, tooth and nail.

Did you think that brutalist
derived from BRUT?
Throw out the Prefects with their plugs!
Let the fun begin!

The Asset

When he shows up alone, in profile, in a hotel room
with curtains drawn and just one lamp switched on,
you wonder where he's been till now and what he's up to
in the semi-dark with three days' worth of stubble –
downing vodka from the mini-bar, casing the bible
in the bedside drawer, unscrewing body-gels
and lotions, taking innocent showers?

He's dressed to kill: black polo-neck, black jeans,
a flash of lilac sock the wardrobe mistress hoped
might lend him depth and personality.
When he stands up to twitch the curtains back
it's always night outside with drifts of rain or snow
caught in the headlights of a prowling van.
Bad weather is the only element he knows.

The briefcase on the chair contains his gun,
long-barrelled, gleaming, oiled, which he takes out
and fondles, ramming on the telescopic lens,
teasing the trigger with slow-motion skill, setting
his sights on one rear window in the block of flats
across the road and then – a cut, a zoom, a jump –
and now he's on the move/the stairs/the roof/the fire escape,

bullets are bouncing off the walls/floors/windows/
shop-fronts/car-doors/kerbs, and you're no longer sure
which side he's on or whether he'll get paid,
and when the credits roll you can't help noticing
he's vanished without trace – not one hot lead
to tie him to the plot, no tell-tale print, no name
or number listed in the cast. Of course there's not.

Party Girl

No one was sure how old she was when she died:
she'd fiddled with passports and portraits, blurred
the dates on marriage-lines and family tree.
Easier to tot up dead bottles or units of alcohol.
The doctors said her lungs would do the trick
(shortness of breath, collapsing airways, painstaking
suffocation). She fancied something more exotic:
her tank of oxygen exploding as she lit another
cigarette. No surprise that she mistook the hospital
for a hotel or that her final words were neither
resignation nor repentance nor dismay
but 'Pour me a gin and tonic would you darling',
as if at last she'd been invited to a proper party
where spirits gurgled like the Styx
and Marlboros came piled high in silver boxes
and she could live it up till break of day.

Resolutions

Determine to go beyond determination,
to give up waiting in the grass for the next
falling leaf. Don't follow the hedging
thrush or the water-rat so circumspect
he'll starve in a scuttle of mud.
Make all your details visible. Wave
bare arms at the sky like Bolle's poplar.
Take yourself for a run in the park
like a white ferret creaming past squirrels
or a psychedelic centaur flashing
pink hooves and purple withers
at the labradors on leads. Resolve
to startle, to stand out, to outrage
like the scream of the jay's blue feather
charging the faint heart of the day.

Michael and Nancy

Clouds brood over the Heath. She runs through the grass
like silverpoint, like speed lassoing its tail, here, there,
gone before my eyes reach the last
place I imagined I saw her, feet off the ground
flirting with notions of wind, air, freedom, flight, ghosts.

In the café she crouches by his chair, shadow ready to spring,
something medieval in her stillness, the narrow skull,
the spine's buttons fastening the drawn skin.
A tourist asks: *Un lévrier?* From *lièvre* for hare.
He shakes his head, *A whippet*, gives it a Gallic spin.

Nancy sits on his lap sipping water from his cupped hand.
He bites an apple, feeds her straight from his mouth.
I'm jealous, half in love with dog and man
like an artist falling for his models, if only I could paint,
find line and colour to describe the tenderness that hangs

so quietly between them – no, more than tenderness
it's *rapture*, from the Middle French, a snatch, a carrying off
from earth to underworld or paradise.
But who's the abductor here, the man with the leash
or the beautiful collared dog with searching eyes?

Cliffhanger

It's not the peaks that haunt him
but those sheer crevasses, couloirs
written white between the rocks,
cauls of angled ice that coffin
those who lose their grip and fetch up
hard against sky-glass, breath
splintered on their lips, gloves
ripped off too late to scratch in snow
the last thought crystallizing
in their clouded eyes – where he,
confronting them like nighthawks
pressed to panes of steamy restaurants,
might find the answer to his question:
are they looking in, or out?

Saintfield

Death visits in its winter form:
Blade-Running rain and the trees unravelling.
Fresh oyster-shells resist the roadside management.

Prophets sleep on the steps of the New Age
wrapped in their beards, dreaming of must-have plasma
and Afternoon Delight from 4 to 7.

Ezekiel, jet-lagged but jaunty
races over the bridge to the lake,
practising the sounds the city has forgotten.

Only the addicts and the bandaged elms remember
the first language –
prayer-beads, carillons, ivory Madonnas.

When will the last leaf fall? When will the earth
give back the scent of guelder-rose and lily?

View from the top

Up here everything's scraped and peeled,
too raw for lint or scab. Doors squeal, floors
send me skidding. The velux sky hangs
granite towers and grated clouds, quivers
with hailstones and referendum blow-out.
There's sulphur in the pipes, a man
screaming 'shoot me!' in the street below.
No space for cushions or curtains, all brink
and cant – cold glass, angled steel, fridge
banging shins, each bruise and callus
keeping me alive. O save me from sinking
and settling, from a past that coddles me
in habits like my mother, always
on the doorstep, holding out my winter coat.

Summer in Marseille

Light consumes its own shadows,
palms whishing away the sun.
Buildings detach and swirl
like egg whites smoking in water.
Beggars ripen. Armpits open
their stoned fruit. The girl waiting
by the stage-door deconstructs
her rose and settles for a selfie
with the poster. Everyone's surly –
sailors, couriers, broadband engineers
with their declarations of conformity,
even the cheese behind tinted glass,
even the still-life with syringes,
gooseberries and one dead bee.
Heat drums on every shell; lethargy
is not an option. The city's sweating.
Can't you see we are all at stake?

Before the Revolution

Flies lay eggs on resting meat as grief feeds on
honey and pistachios, fidgets with the split shells,
the sudden flesh obscenely green. The women
stroke and pinch. Pomegranates dripping
in a white bowl smirk like wounds. This is not
my tragedy: my respects are consumed
by boiled sweets. Legs stick out in so much black,
silences in so much weeping. Cars whisper
over rugs laid out in the street, smudging birds
and flowers. Heat soaks up cola, musk, anguish
in the folds of the neck. The television stays on
in the corner of the room, consoling the blind,
the demented, the young, the believers in magic.

A Couple of Pops

for Hector Gifford

In this scenario knives bend and guns
are happy to see you. The heavies
show up in brogues and tweed,
their fathers' blazing ties, their mothers' hats.

Revenge wears stripy trunks
and *un chapeau de paille*,
chews Love Hearts and Skittles,
shoots from the lip.
Irony's on the move in a fast car
but where oh where is Mister Noir?

Eyeless in St Tropez, straw
down his throat, wasted
on Fruit-Smack and Cremola Foam,
flip-flops raising Cain.
He'll pin the hero to the wall
but hold the Heinz and check
the crimson bubble in the moll's left eye.

Has no one told him blood's
the Real Thing? Has no one told him
life's a stretch of grubby sand
where redemption never comes into focus
and everyone dies in spades?

Tipping Point

Small change – pocketed for taxis or Twixes
or the Cypriot shampooing his hair
or the Poles lifting his sofa up a tower of stairs –
dropped on the 243 to Redvers Road.
It rolls under the seats in front:
wrinkled stockings, downtrodden shoes.
He settles for the power not to look and not to care.

It's only a pound, not worth the fuss.
But the passengers put themselves out, shifting
and bending.   Five apples, says one.
A kilo of onions, adds her friend. Or best potatoes.
It's round here somewhere, give us
a chance. His stop: he can't afford to wait.
He jumps, leaving his satisfaction on the bus.

Reading about the Solar Revolution

for Keith Barnham and Claire Crowther

Dear Keith, I hope your book will help me understand
how sunlight falling in a single hour on earth
can meet the energy demands of humankind
for a whole year, if only leaves give up the secrets
every one of them has always known. I want
to learn, I want to care. I've read your introduction

but it's getting late now and my mind is like a dying planet
so I'll save the unsustainables till morning when it's
light again, and sit here in the darkening garden
dwelling on Claire's unclouded eyes and golden
hair, imagining how it feels to be somebody's
sun, to be somebody's burning answer.

Year of the Rabbit

We spent all summer on the rooftop terrace
waiting for our lives to roll.
The radio promised boys who'd scorch our highways,
shake us to the ground.

Days smelt of musk and vinyl.
Tarmac steamed.
The workmen flashing pipes wore hopsack flares,
their spines like ripening corn under their tans.

The future was calling, calling,
but nowhere in sight.
We turned ourselves like steaks, believing
in the white stripes of watch-straps and bikinis.

If anyone had said the sun would be the end of us
we would have shivered in the midday glare
then slicked our skin with baby-oil
and let it burn.

Le canard pressé

Our duck arrives in a tin coffin,
naked, goose-bumped, crick-necked, head
tucked under its wing.

Every last bit will make it to the table:
liver, breast, crackled skin,
thighs flashing in a frisée frill,

carcass pressed until bones crunch and juices run
while Andrew mans the helm
like John Wayne in a submarine.

Feathers lend support
stuffing the Marilyn cushions on our seats.
The wall frieze bristles with blades.

And all too soon the duck, our dedicated duck,
is a ghost duck, a Proustian revenant,
everything consumed but the beak

which for all we know will go on quacking
long after we're wasted, long after
Otto retires and the heart-shaped lights go out.

Blind Dates

i

Whose unear'd womb disdains the tillage of his husbandry?

William Shakespeare, The Sonnets

Check out his belt, then count the notches on it,
growing like age-rings on a trunk, each crude
encounter ticked off by his tool. I'm not a prude
but all his talk of breeches, petticoats & bonnets
shed for a crook'd potato-finger spoils the mood.
I came for buds & larks; I wanted to be wooed
with velvet leaves & wandering barks & meadows blued
by streams & violets dim. To think that I shampooed
my locks for tales of C's & U's & T's he's viewed.
I'll cut him off with three lines still to run. Begone! It
were no crime to spare the world another fucking sonnet.

ii
The only things we believe in are the sheep and the dogs (Henry James)

Sergeant Troy, Far from the Madding Crowd *by Thomas Hardy*

He flourished his sword by way of introduction, rustling towards
      the hollow among the ferns.
Brass and scarlet shone, the ring of sheep-bells followed. Young and trim,
      by turns
serious and twinkling, he spoke of love but thought of dinner, and though
      I took him
for a wild scamp and a sinner, his well-shaped moustache agitated me
      strangely
until I grew feverish under the evolutions of his blade. He hinted – I
      forbade. Finally
all was over: quick as electricity, he made a hole in my heart that his tongue
could not mend. I did not flinch at his loose play or soldierly démarche.
      Ah, Beauty,
bravely borne! said he, pretending to pay though always intending to owe.
      Yet truth
is truth at any hour of day. The ground was harsh, the haggard night dim
      and starless.
Dogs barked, meek lambs bleated as he fled, but still his sword strung
lanterns in the air and left me shuddering in the streams of his
      aurora militaris.

iii

Eek, ik, eeik, ik, eek

Piet Hanema, Couples *by John Updike*

High sun over the treacherous game, pink lemonade beside his chair, with strawberries, like his mother used to make.

I serve. He crouches at the net, feeling the land around him, sniffing for lust and floods, the racket sweating like a hammer in his fist.

Blood broods under the pale furred legs, the shadow ready to spring. Freckles bounce on his forearms. He plays like a handyman, distracted by upright supports and copper plumbing, testing joints with his knife,

something flat about him, like a greenhouse pane or an honest plaster wall.

We take a break for gin-and-Bitter-Lemon. Advantages shift. He does a handstand on the court, then slaps my behind. Horrid slippery little man who'd eat up every woman in sight and wants the world to lick his hands and find him funny when he's pissed.

He whacks the ball towards death's long canal, bragging that he's second-rate at this, a russet hamster running in his wheel. Who made the cage he's worked so hard not to inherit? Who? Who?

Lousy at love fifteen. He rejoices in the keenness of our chemistry, our symmetry, his stiffening sense of sin. This is God's playground; he won't be mocked.

There's a wife, of course, who guards his soul,

and a snug house and a solemn tugging cookie-faced daughter. He wants to fling me down on the service line till I concede the set. He wants to sleep with me to bring his mother back to life

but he's wondering, from the height of his fear, if I'm a customer whose whims he must work with or a body too rotten to screw.

I can see he's trouble, this small sad shaggy red-haired Dutch boy, watching out for seepage, plugging every hole.

iv

Libertine

Giacomo Casanova, The Memoires of Casanova *by Jacques Casanova de Seingalt*

His chestnut wig could not disguise his age, nor wit his rage: the soup
was too hot, the macaroni cooked in the wrong style, the codfish
too glutinous. Without blushing, he confessed his delight
in losing the right path and indulging his coarse tastes. He wished
me to *know him thoroughly*: each explicit surge and droop
of his passion. He quoted Horace and Homer ad nauseam
while his talons plucked the ribbons at my waist and his dull sight
groped my shoulders and my pretty foot. Unwilling to be the dupe
of a vile lecher, I sharpened his grey lust by rationing my charms
and barring my temple for three hours or more. Near midnight
he gave way to fatigue and dropped off, grunting, in my rigid arms.

v

My feelings will not be repressed

Fitzwilliam Darcy, Pride and Prejudice *by Jane Austen*

We met at the appointed hour and I went boldly on with him alone.
Not all his cleverness could save him from manners lacking
in civility and a face with hardly a good feature. To this discovery
succeeded others equally disagreeable: a critical eye and heavy
blemishes; no cordial feelings or language; a rapid imagination
that jumped from balls to intercourse, giving a loose to his fancy.
My opinion was swiftly decided. I resolved to send him packing
after a few formal inquiries and awkward pauses, but I own
that his pride had stirred resentment so I set the record straight:
'You are not handsome enough for me to consider shacking
up with you, even for ten thousand pounds and a large country estate.'

vi

The Little Tippler

Emily Dickinson

A summer's day – a pretty inn –
A sky of molten blue –
The prospect of wild nights to crown
Our happy rendezvous –

Her sparkling eyes – her heady grin –
Her talk of drams and tipples –
Sweetest success! – I order gin –
A double – then a triple –

My love's on tap – it froths like beer –
Her virtue's anecdotal –
But – O – 'tis air she sips – I fear
She's vestal and teetotal.

He always gets the new girl

Don Draper, Mad Men *by Matthew Weiner*

I'll paint you a picture: crisp shirt, thin tie, molten gold in an old-fashioned glass.

He smokes all the time but, man, is he good with the words! Is there always a party?

He likes oceans, bridges, Valentina in *La Notte*. Sugar cubes crushed with a compact, hearts of palm.

Love is his slogan: he pours it neat and wrings it dry. Takes the afternoon off, lies on his couch making boredom the contract everyone needs to sign.

He has a reputation. What do I want him to say? He's looking for a girl to keep him straight, someone between a mother and a maid, candy for his crooked arm.

He kisses like a heel but he's funny, kind of, paddling along on his raft of bitters and rye.

My God, he drawls, *Stop talking. How does room service sound?*

Like pain from an old wound.

He'll never change. He'll die alone, under his rock, and never feel a thing, sour-breathed, wine-stained, still dreaming hope is sentences away, stuck in the elevator between two shiny floors.

Summer's coming, he says. He'll pull it out of thin air. How stupid does he think I am? He'll smash my cherry, then just plop it in. Who'll care? Not the city, not the world.

This meeting's over. I hate to break it to him but tomorrow's not for sale. *Him* feeling something – that would sell.

viii

When the real spring comes

Oliver Mellors, Lady Chatterley's Lover *by D H Lawrence*

I came down the steps and there he was at the bar before me,
So dark and so cocksure, solitary and intent,
His face inscrutable under the heavy brows, his cheekbones showing.
And he lifted his head from his drinking and looked at me through a
       bellyful of remembering,
His hand on the table, loose and forgotten, like a sleeping dog.
For a moment we were together in the flood; he could have washed my
       soul transparent.
Then, as if a wind tossed him, he got up and came to me and I saw the
       black days ahead,
The complications and the ugliness and his heart as cold as cold potatoes,
And my blood sank and I did not quite dare to let him take me home.
But afterwards I regretted it, and voices in me said I had missed my chance
       with tenderness
And would have to light my little flame alone.

ix

How Sir Launcelot was to-fore the door of the chamber

Launcelot du Lake, Le Morte D'Arthur, *by Thomas Malory*

Before he pulled off his helm, I weened he was Sir Launcelot du Lake,
      a knight
wifeless and lecherous, noised to love the Queen, to take his pleasaunce
      with paramours
and spend his days in jousts and deeds of arms, putting better kemps
      than he to flight.
And yet he proffered me courtesy and gentleness and promised to fulfil
      all my desires
and intents. Nay, truly he seemed the flower of all men. Our chamber
      richly dight,
said he, 'Fair Damosel, I am no ravisher of women, nor foul churl
      who doth shame
to my order. As I am true knight of the Table Round, I had liefer die
      than grieve
you.' So saying, his helm he laid under his head and rested him long
      with play and game.
Yea, on my very life I would have let him wield me, yet he had lust
      to sleep perforce
and when day shone, made I great sorrow and was passing heavy
      as he took his leave
for I was ready to go with him wherever he would have me
      but alas I had no horse.

We are not meant for happiness

Maxim de Winter, Rebecca *by Daphne du Maurier*

Two slices of bread and butter each, and China tea,
a snowy cloth, gingerbread, floury scones, crumpets
melting in the mouth, a little table drawn before the fire.
He smoked, I ate. Women are not like men, we take
our chances when we can. He stared at me moodily
wrapped in his secret self. Oh, that dark, lost look of his,
those wounded eyes, the face swept cold and clean.
He belonged in a different century, in a walled city
with winding streets and twisted spires. His cigarettes
told a smouldering truth. I sliced more angel cake.
He seized the ashtray, stubbing out desire.

xi

On ne peut croire ce qui ne se comprend pas

Pierre Abélard, Letters of Abelard and Heloise *by Pierre Bayle*

I would not have suspected him for a doctor by his dress
though who can resist the brilliance of a man whose faculties
confound the learned of his age? His person is advantageous
enough; he is formidable in logic and his conversation displays
the precepts of Ovid and the weapons of dialectic. His genius
attracts my vanity. Even the most trivial of his verses
will last as long as there are lovers in this world. Were I his mistress
he would raise me to the character of a goddess, yet (I confess
my inconsistency without a blush) it is sometimes dangerous
to have too much merit. He dotes on solitude and difficulties,
his chalice holds a bitter draught. I have no use for such austerities.

xii

The only cause he knows

Rhett Butler, Gone with the Wind *by Margaret Mitchell*

In he strides, lips curled, black boots flashing – hot yam,
I'm in love! Moths in my gut, knots in my throat, all at sea
on a tide of tongues. He's swarthy as a pirate, varmint eyes, floppy
fringe, tomcat grin, cool way with a pork rib, and soon drammed
up on Southern Comfort. I swallow all his riddles with sweet tea.
Beneath the scars he claims he's soft as a shimmy, soppy
about ponies and puppies, squishy to the core, proud to wheel a pram.
He swears he'll set me up in Maryland or Tennessee,
revamp my life with barbecues and cotton. O Mammy, what a ham!
It wouldn't last. He'll always be a wham-bam-
thank-you man. He can't convince me that he gives a damn.

xiii

Fairy-tale Prince

Cinderilla or The Little Glass Slipper *by Charles Perrault*

Let it be proclaimed by sound of trumpet: the Prince was charming.
He handed me out of the coach, led me gracefully through the hall
to the most honourable seat, then took me out to join the dancing.
A lavish collation was served, of which he ate not one morsel
so intently did he load me with amorous and disarming
compliments about my silks, jewels, ankles, *belle*
coiffure, his gaze busy on my dress. When he fell to palming
the border of my thighs, I understood why scholars concur
that the slipper I left behind was made not of glass, but of fur
and stood for the sheltered kingdom on which he was advancing,
whipping his lusty stallion, waving his *droit de seigneur*.

xiv

A little chapter, in which is contained a little incident

Tom Jones *by Henry Fielding*

He accosted me with some of the ordinary forms of salutation, which I in the same manner returned and our conversation began on the delicious beauty of the fine house and land.

Before we proceeded farther, he acquainted me that he intended to digress as often as he saw occasion, assuring me there would be nothing in his demeanour inconsistent with the strictest rules of decency.

He had little sobriety in his countenance, and a propensity to many vices, yet bad as he was, he must serve as the heroe of this history.

We walked forth and our talk past swiftly to matters of a different kind from those preceding: despite the virtuous love he bore another,

he claimed I had taken his heart by surprize and the rest of his body had a right to follow.

Reader, take care: nothing is more irksome than to be at one's own expense the object of an honest man's pleasure.

Both his looks and his voice were full of tenderness, and he produced extravagant effects augmented by wine, then, laying aside all allegory, snatched and kissed my hand.

You may see that his nature was as difficult to be met with as a sausage from Bologna, yet, though his animal spirits may be condemned, by some, as unnatural, my business is only to record the truth.

Therefore, lest anything offend in the perusal, I am obliged to choak my reflections and contemplate the weather.

Suffice to say, the evening breeze was sweet, but he had led me to the top of a hill, and how to get me down without breaking my neck, he knew not. However deficient in outward tokens of respect, he was such a pretty fellow

I gladly feasted at his table of love, and afterwards we slid down together.

Drunk on Words

Dylan Thomas

He's on his thirteenth whisky, blubbery lips on the holy rim
as the Sabbath's wild bells dwindle over the harbour wall. Unlucky for some.
Bombastic barfly, gabbling, cod-tough in the sneering, moley light,
drawling, sprawling, livery, dock-bound by infidelities, pausing to shout
at the sea, the white-horsed tide and the rain-wringing tongues of the
        headlong night,
green now and bloated, sonorous as Satan, a fierce-eyed opium-eater
        singing tunes
to the landlord's cruel-whiskered cat. Beast, angel, madman
who can't read Welsh and swears he writes sober in the mewling dawn!
I still don't know, and never will, why I'm here at all, but I let him
begin at the beginning, under the stars falling cold and the fabled moon
which will kill him so easily, all but one of his fires already out.

Rilke in Venice

In love again, trailing through the rain
to another damp church, another
gloomy Tintoretto.

It's all been said before:
marbled air, brittle palazzos,
water dripping like feathers,
angel-faces at the wells.

Here's Goethe staring out to sea
pondering the ebb and flow of life,
Palladio with his ruler, Titian opening
eyes, Turner blinded by the sun,
Aschenbach simply embarrassing.

Watch the processions in the pink light,
ghosts in their carnival masks,
prisoners on the Bridge of Sighs,
all the jaunty little boats drawn
to the cemetery island,
its black trees, its cracked tombs.

We are not finished with each other yet.
The past's red coat
runs through the dark flashing knives.

Ruskin's Rhetoric of Rain

To say the sky is grieving would be false –
the sky can show no sympathy for me –
yet nothing illustrates my sense of loss
quite like pathetic fallacy.

The day is overcast, but not benighted.
The wind sighs not for me, but through the trees.
The clouds are heavy, but not heavy-hearted.
They frown on elegy.

The sky is grey because I cannot see the blue.
These drops that prick my cheeks can be explained.
The wet rose in the garden is not you.
My mind has made it rain.

The statue drips, but does not wring its hands.
The flowers droop and break, but feel no pain.
The willows weep, but cannot understand
you will not come again.

Sunshine may follow, but the transient rays
are just a fanciful motif.
Life is pathetic, love's a fallacy.
The cruel rain cannot contain my grief.

Translating Proust

'Longtemps, je me suis couché de bonne heure.'

Thirty pages to describe how he tossed and turned in bed before
he fell asleep, the hours stretching from *long*
to *temps* like smoke from the snuffed candle, the match struck
at midnight in a lost hotel. Lights out early,
the sound of minutes scratched away in the room downstairs:
creaking woodwork, the shifting darkness of tables and oil lamps,
rumours of gold under the door.
A lifetime's habits dusted off on the fresh cheeks of his pillow,
the past and its countries flashed back by spinning walls
and stiffened limbs, whispers of muslin along the hall.
High ceilings, insolent clocks, the pitiless mirror,
the window over the street – all there in that first word,
conspiring with memory to resist translation.

The Art of Translation: Mouth-to-Mouth

First, clear your throat and swallow hard,
then carefully unlatch his larynx. Take note
of the interior design – the bric-a-brac,
the prints, the views, the room at the top
where he squats in the shadows spitting static.

No point expecting him to shake your hand,
switch on the lights or introduce you to his pets.
There'll be no custard creams or jasmine tea.
You'll learn to play dead or play dumb,
to go down on your knees and pay court
while he sharpens his pen
and scratches his thoughts on your tongue.

Sonnet in X

after Mallarmé

Midnight in the empty salon, and Misery Jane
is sky-high already, flashing onyx
fingernails in the lamplight, her darkling brain
full of horny dreams torched by the Phoenix

into ash that has no shelf-life in a ptyx
or any echoing curio from the ocean's drain
(as The Master's out drawing tears from the Styx
with the only shell the Void does not disdain).

But near the blank north window, the gold mixed
for a backdrop of unicorns trying to inflame
a mermaid is flaking fast, and in the mirror's pane,

all skin and bones, given the deep six, here she is again
with seven forgotten stars caught in same frame,
twinkling and flickering through the realms of Nyx.

After Goethe

Versions of *Wandrers Nachtlied II*

Wearily Romantic

How restful it is
In the hills,
So still
At the tops of the trees,
Scarcely a breeze,
Little birds hushed in their nests.
Wait a while,
Soon you can rest.

Ec(h)o

Up here in the hills
it's so still:
trees everywhere
struggling
for air,
birds falling silent in the parks.
All you can hear, a whistling
in the dark.

QT

hilltops
decrescendo
treetops
diminuendo
ppp
birds dumb

keep mum
RIP

Mis-reading

The peace summits
are over.
In the hurly-burly
you toe the line,
barely breathing.
Shuttlecocks are squashed
        in the woods.
It's only a viewpoint. Any minute now
they'll shut you up for good.

Joseph Cornell and a Craving for Chocolate

In the blue hours, yearnings
for French hotels and German forests:
the brain as Wunderkammer or Swiss cheese,
honeycombed and lockered,
dimples in thimbles and shells,
de Chirico windows, Mondrian maps.
Who's counting the cells?

He still has all his marbles
but Flaubert in a nightcap
warns him not to touch his idols
lest the gold dissolve.

He harbours chocolate squares,
neat rows of pralines indexed like stones.
Thoughts flutter like doves
or moths or ballerinas' pumps:
fly-paper trapping hope in padded rooms.
Fossils, atlases, stars,
compasses, mountains, sand.

Imagination is a tap to turn off cravings.
Who needs to arrive?
Who needs to visit friends in Europe?

Memories cloak his tongue –
dust on his lips, the slow
melt, the velvet slide.
He dwells on swallowed loss.

Elizabeth Bishop's Toucan

What sex was he? She never knew
but like the subjects of her early poems
she made him male. Sammy was black
or most of him was black, with dabs
of neon brilliance: eyes electric-blue,
huge bill greenish-yellow/bluish-green,
a bunch of scarlet plumes blazing
like a sunset under his tail.

He loved bright things – the cat's
wet nose, diamonds, rings, shiny centavos
tossed for him to catch. He stole toast
from her plates, corks from her bottles,
swaggered off cackling like a witch.
She used to wash him with the garden hose
or fill a basin several inches deep
and watch him plunge and splash
until his skin flashed through
like denim under ceremonial robes.

Left in the rain he'd stretch out
straight as a stick, his beak erect,
Brancusi's *Bird in Flight*.

Six years later he was poisoned
by insecticide for treating fleas.
She found him lying in his cage, feet
in the air, 'most comical of all in death'.

She blamed herself, took to her bed,
devoured the cook's consoling gingerbread,
then tried – for years – to write
an ode to him, dear funny Uncle Sam,
searching for words to launch him

back into the light, flapping, flying, flown,
rising on her breath
towards the sun's irresistible coin.

Earl Grey and Auerbach

Drinking tea by long windows framing the slide into dusk
the mute Thames gliding through the swollen city
buildings opening into nets of their solids
no near no far no there no here
everything lumped and pressed in the same plane
bright waver of moon riding vertical horizons
everything heavily present
as if we could divide by ten and still confront
the same immanent experience the same impasto
squeezed from a fresh tube moments ago
while tea leaves coloured the water
and steam curled slowly over a view so shining wet
so charged and viable we'd push our fingers
through the glass to feel its pulse and flux

Vincent in Manitoba

He would have painted the sunflowers of course,
yellows so intense the air hazed gold
and pollen dusted his skin. And the cobbled blue sky
wheeled into flames by the sulphur glow. And the clouds,
the clouds – wadding for every barn in Altona –
clouds clouds clouds
as if the fields themselves were breathing.
Kind Margruite would have lent him
her brushes and oils, her wooden chair, her studio
hollowed in the eaves, frame-windows drawing in
the aching land, the bluffs of poplar and oak fringed
copper by the wind. And the crows exploding
like bats from the wheat, trashing the horizon
with their shrieks. Poor scarecrow flagging
in his woollen coat and fur-brimmed hat,
he would have stared till light crazed his tongue,
stared at what he knew was truth –
the shapes of pain thrown wet on the canvas,
the sunflowers blackened, hanging their heads.

Dover Beach Revisited

Life's a beach. Enough to know
the sea will break, and break, and break, and break again
along the shore, the shore, the shore, the shore, the shore.

A Pinch of Heaney

He came with the wind, strode like a Norse god
through the bog of my dream, boots steeped in mud,
all night scuffling at my shoulder
plucking roots and clods from the furrows of my verse,

hacking at the soft pulp, clearing each foot
so he could scatter obsidian and chert
which showered the page like sparks
from a silver-tongued strimmer hoisting plain silage

into the marvellous. I woke to a clean yard:
no spade, no hazel-sticks, no neat-stacked turf.
Beyond the hedgerow, gales of laughter
and the scrabbled earth.

Dress-down Day in the Privy Garden

Since curtseys have been dropped she stands among the daisies
knotted by box. He comes alone. Petals bleed over the grass,
leaves bruise at his command. He does not wear his crown.
She is told to raise her shift and think of England.

Now ravens make short work of all the pretty finches flocking
to her window. It is said the Thames will run dry
and ripening grapes will shrivel on their stems and every rose
in the land blacken and fall prey to beetles.

Willows write her sentence on the wall. She knows he prays for her soul.
She knows there is nothing he would not do to release her.
She has heard his heart sing under its thatch
but still she cannot tell string from rope or yoke from beating wing.

Exhibition

You knew the background.
I pretended, blurring
names and dates. Were they
Borgias or Gonzagas?
You would have furnished details
had I stooped to ask:
intrigues, betrayals,
whisperings in gilded halls.

It's all history now, the oils
returned to shuttered chambers
in a dozen hilltop towns.
And who's to say
the face you wore that day
is less worth nailing up as art
than heads of dynasties
I should have recognized
but never had by heart.

Scenes from Dürer's Marriage

He could draw a face like no one else on earth,
each crow's foot, fin of ear and snail-line hair
so perfect that you reach to touch
but when it comes to breasts
you wonder if he ever saw one in the flesh.

His Eves grow apples plumper than forbidden fruit.
His mermaids hanging by the scruff
from Maximilian's Arch are fine on paper
if you like your game-birds high.
But bosoms? Theirs are cannon-balls,
cathedral domes, imperial helmets, multi-view
projections, inward synthesis for Kinder Eggs.

Poor Agnes had her glands constructed
through abbreviation or laid bare
in fractions of her total height
but never mastered with a feeling hand.
Perhaps he loved her more for her proportions
than her charms, catching her in nets
that cooled his heart but ruled his pen.
Perhaps he never looked at her
behind drawn curtains.

Bedding Down

Strindberg's second marriage, to Frida Uhl, Heligoland, May 1893

It's all so sudden – she's like a seed
dropped by a bird, sunk deep in sand,
keening for rain. Traditional landscape
of hills and trees, a quiet river flowing past.
Then in a flash it's New Year and here
he is, cracking her in his hand.

Another will call it spring awakening,
this flood of love that needs no banns.
Three days of peace, barely time to bed down.
Is this marriage on the rocks?
He walks above the tide, gulls in his eyes.
She pays for food and board with blood.

Looking back, she sees him salted
to a red colossus, dredging gold
from the black breakers, the curdled air, the cliff
face, the torch-flowers – while she turns on
light after light in room after room,
gunning for the brilliance of the sun.

Strindberg in Love

It must end terribly –
a mallet falling on happiness,
chairs pushed back from the table.

Light is not his destiny.
If only the damned summer were over.
He'd be happy for it to be winter
all year round.

Incredible Labour

Mary Shelley dreams the monster, 16 June 1816

They were already calling it *The Year without a Summer*:
rain dashing against my windows hour after hour,
the sky so ashen and confused I could not see the lake
though it was said to shine phosphoric like the sea.

The world was full of negatives: no crops, no radiant energy,
no flights of the imagination. Snow in Italy fell red,
in Hungary brown. Dark spots on the sun's disk
announced the extinction of nature and the end of days.

Each morning he asked me, *Have you? Have you?*
Have you thought of a story?
Dear Lord, so keen to keep us all amused!
He never slept without a pair of pistols by his side.

At noon the earth swung blind and fowls hid in the trees.
I read by the despairing light of candles
or listened to the thunder in the others' minds:
L'Heure Fatale, La Chambre Grise, La Tête de Mort.

Awake at night I gave suck to my dead baby. If only
I could find the instruments of life! Galvanism
had given token of such things but moonlight struggled
to get through. How could I write, no longer a mother now?

Heartache and headaches; convulsive, half-vital motion.
The tumour grew fat inside me, feeding on abnormalities
until words kicked their way out, shrivelled, bloodied things
that soiled my midnight pillow but lost their currency

when Fanny killed herself – and Harriet drowned –
and my two children died – and Percy's corpse washed up
like a pearly fish – and I expelled another foetus six years
to the day since I beheld the awful product of my toils.

Lightning Source UK Ltd.
Milton Keynes UK
UKOW01f2144030417
298237UK00001B/52/P